SIMPLY
CHRISTMAS

★

SIMPLY
CHRISTMAS

★

SHEILA PICKLES

PAVILION

For Tricia Guild, an Inspiration to Us All

FIRST PUBLISHED IN GREAT BRITAIN IN 1994 BY
PAVILION BOOKS LIMITED
26 UPPER GROUND
LONDON SE1 9PD

TEXT COPYRIGHT © 1994 BY SHEILA PICKLES
ADDITIONAL TEXT BY ELIZABETH WILHIDE
COMMISSIONED PHOTOGRAPHS COPYRIGHT © 1994 BY TONY AMOS
FOR OTHER PHOTOGRAPHIC CREDITS, SEE PAGE 120
PHOTOGRAPHIC STYLING BY SAM TODHUNTER
PICTURE RESEARCH BY EMILY HEDGES

THE MORAL RIGHT OF THE AUTHOR HAS BEEN ASSERTED

DESIGNED BY DAVID FORDHAM

A CIP CATALOGUE RECORD FOR THIS BOOK IS AVAILABLE FROM THE
BRITISH LIBRARY

ISBN 1-85793-159 9

PRINTED AND BOUND IN ITALY BY NEW INTERLITHO
TYPESET IN FUTURA BY DORCHESTER TYPESETTING GROUP LTD

2 4 6 8 10 9 7 5 3 1

THIS BOOK MAY BE ORDERED BY POST DIRECT FROM THE PUBLISHER. PLEASE
CONTACT THE MARKETING DEPARTMENT. BUT TRY YOUR BOOKSHOP FIRST.

CONTENTS

INTRODUCTION

WHEN I WAS A CHILD, living in a small village on the edge of the Yorkshire moors, Christmas was a time of tradition. Every year a large fir tree stood in the corner of the hall, decorated with strands of multicoloured fairy lights and trimmed with bright glass ornaments. After school finished for the holidays, we kept ourselves busy making cards, colouring, cutting and gluing paper to make chains, watching with barely controlled excitement as the pile of presents under the tree grew higher and higher. We listened to carols, strung the cards we had received on ribbons to hang down the walls and cut branches of holly and ivy to decorate mantelpieces and windowsills all over the house.

It cost little, for we made use of what grew in the garden and what we found in the woods, and every year we brought out the old familiar ornaments which had been handed down in the family for generations to embellish the tree. It never occurred to us that Christmas could be celebrated any other way. We travelled little and had no acquaintance with customs other than our own.

Unchanging from year to year, our Christmases were comforting and reassuring, but no less special for that. It does not take long for a tradition to become planted in the mind of a child and for my own children today Christmas would be unthinkable without a tree or the paper decorations they have painstakingly created in previous years.

Christmas has a pattern of its own, enshrined in the familiar succession of festivities we know and love. From the magical anticipation of Christmas Eve through to the revelries of Twelfth Night, each day of the celebration has its own special flavour. Many of the customs and rites associated with the season are much more ancient than we realize.

In the centuries preceding Christianity, pagan religions marked the point of midwinter with feasting and ceremony. The Roman festivals of Saturnalia and

THE four main sections of this book – Natural, Gold, White and Colour – reflect the most popular approaches to Christmas decorating. Decorating to a theme is stylish, sophisticated and fun. Choose whichever suits your own lifestyle and complements your surroundings. Within each broad category, there is infinite scope for variation and experiment, and a host of imaginative ideas for gift-wrapping, displays, table settings and trimming the tree.

Kalends and the Yuletide celebrations of northern Europe all took place around the time of the winter solstice and the turn of the year, commemorating the beginning of a new cycle of fertility and growth. Evergreen was revered because it symbolized the continuity of life at a time when all of nature seemed dormant. Light and fire were sacred, in honour of the rebirth of the sun. Feasting, revelry and gift-giving brought cheer to the dark, cold days of winter.

In medieval times, many of these pagan traditions still flourished in the twelve-day festival of Christmas. On the hallowed eve of Christmas, the giant Yule log was ceremonially kindled from a fragment of the Yule log of the previous year and the Yule candle was lit. Medieval halls were decked with branches of holly, yew and laurel and a Christmas bush of greenery hung from the ceiling. The oldest or most productive fruit trees were wassailed to ensure a good harvest for the following year. Everyone ate and drank heartily. Dancing and carol-singing, good fellowship and high spirits reached a climax on Epiphany or Twelfth Night in glorious revels, when mummers' plays were performed, tournaments and contests took place and fanciful disguises were worn. After the partying was over, decorations were taken down and evergreen burned or buried to avoid bad luck.

A Christmas today enshrines many of these ancient customs, together with newer practices which arose comparatively recently in Victorian days. During the time of the Puritans and for quite a long period after, Christmas was a very subdued affair, and the medieval spirit of festivity was all but lost. When Christmas was revived as a family festival at the beginning of the nineteenth century, all the familiar elements we know today were set in place. The German tradition of the Christmas tree was brought to Britain by Prince Albert to become the focus of our celebrations. Christmas cards, pantomime, and even the Christmas cracker all date from this time. St Nicholas made his transformation into the jolly figure of Father Christmas, gladdening the

ENTRANCES set the scene. This winter garland frames a handsome doorway and serves as an evocative introduction to Christmas festivities. The effect is luxurious, but the ingredients are not. Terracotta pots, frosted cones, tied cinnamon sticks, leeks and heads of garlic are displayed against a background of dark fir boughs, for a celebration of nature's bounty.

hearts of children with his sleigh full of gifts. Twelve days of feasting in the medieval manner are well beyond most people's expectations of Christmas today. Even to recreate the Yorkshire Christmas of my childhood would now be an expensive and time-consuming affair in the city, with the demands of work ever-present. Nevertheless, the spirit of Christmas is alive and well all over the world and seasonal festivities and gatherings are still sacrosanct for modern families as they create and maintain their own traditions.

Our family Christmas in London has its own fixed points of celebration – the Nativity play at a local school performed by children in their handmade costumes, carol-singing around the piano on Christmas Eve at the home of our friends, the visit to church for Midnight Mass. After breakfast on Christmas morning, there is the excitement of unwrapping presents; after lunch we always gather to listen to the Queen's broadcast at three. My Christmas would not be complete without the yearly visit of the carol-singers on their rounds, or the Christmas pudding with lucky silver sixpences hidden deep inside. For my children, Christmas means fun making cards and presents, decorating the Christmas cake and, of course, the tree.

If we have lovingly clung to many familiar traditions, there are others which have gone by the board. Some years ago, we cheerfully abandoned the standard Christmas fare of turkey, with its interminable leftovers, in favour of pheasant as the centrepiece of Christmas lunch. At one time, I also used to believe that the whole house needed to be embellished. Every mantelpiece was thick with cards and garlands and every windowsill dressed in greenery. Now I have come to appreciate the virtues of simplicity and the truth of 'less is more'. I have learned that one bowl of beautiful objects in a room gives more pleasure and is more effective, as well as being less demanding in terms of time and cost.

The purpose of this book is to demonstrate how simple decorative ideas can revive and refresh our experience of Christmas and bring new meaning to our cherished traditions. I suspect that many people, regularly overwhelmed by Christmas preparations and burdened with the task of recreating the same effect year after year, approach the holiday season with something akin to dread. Christmas provides us with the opportunity to make a break with the plodding routine of daily life, but if it too becomes a dull and toilsome ritual, the zest and excitement of the season disappears.

Decorating our houses will always be part of the Christmas festivities. It is a time when we welcome family and friends into our homes, gather round the table to eat and drink and mark the passing of another year. Transforming our surroundings with colour and glitter is all part of the celebratory mood.

I believe that Christmas decorating need not involve superhuman effort or crushing expense. The very simplest means can be highly effective at creating a sense of magic and delight. On my travels, I like to search out tiny inexpensive objects in street markets and antique shops – lengths of crushed velvet and brocade to make into tablecloths, buttons and bows from period costumes to decorate crackers and gifts. Nowadays, you needn't travel further than the nearest craft or furnishing shop to discover exotic elements from farflung corners of the globe which will give an original twist to your Christmas decorations. Even city gardens can provide a wealth of natural ingredients for intriguing displays. Most of the ideas in this book are both inexpensive and simple to put together and many can be made by the children, who always enjoy joining in the preparations.

I have always found that the best approach to Christmas decoration is to adopt a theme and carry it through in the decoration of the tree, gift wrapping and table settings. This does not mean adhering to a rigidly coordinated look, which can be deadening and spiritless, but is merely a question of building around a family of colours or ideas for consistency and impact. The main sections of this book – Gold, Colour, White and Natural – reflect the most popular ways of responding to the season, and enable you to choose whichever approach suits your own home and way of life. Gold is rich and bright, ideal for dressing up a stylish city apartment, but it is also grand and sophisticated in a period setting. Bright colour is instantly festive and playful, a theme for exuberant family Christmases in town or country. White brings the glitter and glamour of winter indoors and spells the height of elegance in a contem-

porary home. Natural decorating, with evergreen, fruit, flowers, twigs and leaves, can be rustic and countrified, or beautifully stark and simple.

The focus of most people's decorative efforts remains the tree. Decorating a tree to a theme is dramatically unifying and much more effective than overloading the branches with a jumble of mismatched ornaments, all in different shapes, colours and sizes. If you feel that cutting down large trees for two weeks' amusement represents something of a waste, but equally abhor artificial varieties, you can recreate the same effect in witty displays of twigs or other stylized arrangements.

Another natural place for display is the fireplace, the traditional source of winter warmth and cheer. Garlands twined along a mantelpiece or embellishing a fine mirror frame add a flourish of festive interest. Entrance halls, where guests are welcomed, also call for some decorative touches to mark the season: the wreath is a traditional form of decoration which can be interpreted in a host of original ways. Since many of our Christmas celebrations revolve around food, decorating the table provides a feast for the eyes and an instant sense of glamour and occasion.

It goes without saying that decorations should complement, rather than obliterate the character of your home. It is far better to draw the eye to points of architectural interest, mark the places where people gather, or emphasize a beautiful view, than to cram every nook and cranny with festive trimmings or scatter baubles over every surface. One stunning arrangement, strategically placed, has great drama and presence.

Above all, Christmas decorating should be fun. The simplest ideas, which make elegant use of original materials, are often the most effective, and help to conserve our energies and finances at this busy and inevitably expensive time of the year. The unexpected is always appealing: many of the objects which are part of our everyday lives can be put to work in new combinations with wit and flair.

Without festivities to interrupt the rhythm of the year, life would be depressingly monotonous and dull. Decorating for Christmas is a direct and accessible way of expressing all our joy in the season.

THE Christmas tree is the focus of our celebrations. Introduced by Prince Albert in the nineteenth century, the custom has become one of the most popular and best-loved. Decorated with white gauze bows, glass balls and ornaments, gold pears and suns, this shimmering tree is beautifully at home in the corner of an elegant white drawing room. Positioning a tree near a window creates a delightful view from the street and a heart-warming sight to come home to.

NATURAL

THE NATURAL APPROACH to Christmas decorating is simple and direct. The subtle tones, intriguing shapes and contrasts of texture provided by natural ingredients make enthralling displays that appeal to all the senses. Fruit, flowers, foliage, nuts and seedpods work together in effortless combination and many of the elements can be assembled for next to nothing.

During the year, twigs, leaves, flowers and herbs can be collected from the countryside or garden, dried and stored to be on hand for the Christmas season. These basic materials can be supplemented nearer the time by evergreen boughs, fresh and dried fruit, vegetables, shells, nuts and anything else which takes your fancy. In a spirit of conservation and ecological awareness, dec-orative trimmings can be fashioned from raffia, twists of muslin, leaves and natural fibre papers for a look which is both resourceful and original.

Evergreen holly, pine and mistletoe were revered as symbols of life in ancient winter festivities, an association we continue to mark in the more recent tradition of the Christmas tree. Decorations in plaited straw and raffia feature in the Christmas customs of many northern countries, and all over the world the bounty of the harvest is carefully husbanded and preserved for winter feasts. This is a time when we can be at our most creative and hospitable. Bowls piled high with colourful fruit, sweet-scented garlands and wreaths trimmed with bright berries bring nature indoors to celebrate the season.

GARLANDS are among the most versatile of Christmas decorations. String a garland across a window, loop it over a chair back, hang it above a mantel-piece – or wind it down a staircase – to bring the festive spirit into your home. Natural materials, plentiful, cheap and easy to work with, make excellent ingredients. This delightfully spiky garland combines dried red chillis with the burnished glow of Mexican copper ornaments.

★ Use medium-gauge florist's wire or stout twine for threading the ingredients. Small bunches of fresh chillis wired together can be hung from the tree for a splash of vibrant colour.

WARM frescoed walls make a perfect background for a mantelpiece decoration which evokes the bounty of nature (left). The form of the metal wall sconce is echoed by tied wheatsheaves in an original departure from the usual Christmas greenery. Careful symmetry of design prevents the effect from looking chaotic. A pair of wheatsheaves tied with raffia and packed into terracotta pots with sphagnum moss flank the display. Dried flower heads, including alchemilla mollis, tiny cones and ivy part-sprayed dull gold add points of colour.

★ To create this type of simple garland, bind short boughs of spruce together with florist's wire or garden string and attach to a piece of stout twine or thin rope cut to the required length. Add clusters of cones and gourds at intervals. Cones can be wired in place very easily. To secure a gourd, pierce with wire and twist both ends of the wire together. You can use a glue gun to attach wire to the base of nuts.

A MORE subdued, but no less effective mantelpiece garland (above) mixes blue spruce boughs with pine cones and gourds, the blue-green of the spruce and ochre of the gourds picking up the tones of the Chinoiserie paper and gilt picture frame to give a sophisticated feel.

ELEGANTLY understated, this table setting relies on an evocative combination of natural materials – linen, wood and metal wire – as a foil for exotic treats. The tablecloth by Carolyn Quatermaine is screenprinted with fragments from an eighteenth-century French manuscript and free-hand decoration. A wooden Shaker plate and wire basket hold exotic fruits and 'follovielle'. These traditional Italian sweetmeats consist of raisins or figs, with crystallized orange and lemon peel, baked in lemon leaves – delicious with after-dinner coffee.

★ You can dress your own table with an instant version of the same cloth. Choose plain linen or cheap unbleached calico and decorate with fabric pens or paints. The result is more subtle if you decorate in shades which are close in tone to the cloth. Calligraphy is particularly effective – and if the script is in a foreign language, the decorative shape of the writing is enhanced. The matching linen napkins shown here are simply edged with a plain dotted line of running stitch.

THE WREATH or circle of flowers, fruit, vines or greenery is an ancient symbol of celebration. At Christmas, the wreath holds special significance and traditionally is used to decorate doors and entrances or mark the places where people gather to enjoy the festivities. Wreaths are simple to make and you can have fun experimenting with different combinations of ingredients. And the joy of using natural materials is that much of what you need can be collected free from gardens and woodland: the examples shown here make use of bright winter berries, cones, seedpods, ivy and dried hydrangea heads as well as various forms of evergreen.

★ To make a wreath, first construct a base which is sturdy enough to support the decoration. There are a wide range of materials you can use for bases, including wood, twisted vines built up to form a thick ring, straw or wire; (ready-made bases are available from florists). Plain wire frames can be covered with dense clumps of springy sphagnum moss attached with finer florist's wire for an evergreen base.
The next stage is to cover the base with decorative ingredients. If the base is attractive in its own right, you may not need to add a great deal to it. For a full effect, however, wire on overlapping boughs of greenery to cover the base completely and trim with clumps of berries, seeds or cones.

21

CHOCOLATE asparagus to tempt a food-lover (right) is arranged on a shaped plate set in a shortbread mould, a combination of diverse elements which makes play with shapes to create a sense of occasion. Dried hydrangea heads packed in an old country jug strike a suitably rustic look.

THE NATURAL theme is the inspiration for this novel present idea (left), which makes a virtue of simplicity. A stack of Indian leaf plates forms a base for a wooden dish in the shape of a heart, piled with sugared dried figs. In an original twist, a painted laurel leaf serves as a gift label, tied on with raffia string.

★ Laurel leaves are glossy and robust enough to be written on. Petals and other large leaves such as beech and chestnut can be pressed, sprayed or painted, and then carefully inscribed to make unusual tags.

★ The muted, delicate shades of dried hydrangea add subtlety to winter flower arrangements. If you grow hydrangeas in your garden, you can cut a selection of heads earlier in the year and dry them to enjoy later on. Cut the stems back only as far as the new buds to ensure a good display on the shrub the following year. Arrange the cut heads in a vase with a couple of inches of water and leave them to dry. The addition to glycerine to the water will prevent the petals becoming too brittle.

★ When using fresh flowers to decorate a tree, you can insert each stem into a florist's vial and top up with water to prolong their life.

CONSERVATORIES, greenhouses and garden rooms bring nature closer. Evergreen plants and trees were traditionally revered as symbols of life because their leaves never died. Appropriately, the decoration of this tree (above) lets nature speak for itself and revives the meaning of an age-old association. Decked with garlands of silver-grey foliage, pure white rose heads and shiny metal stars – and to crown it all, a wreath of silvered ivy – this festive tree testifies to the simplicity of a single colour scheme. A stack of brown-paper parcels trimmed with sprays of flowers and leaves pursues the theme.

A VICTORIAN conservatory is transformed into a woodland glade for evocative Christmas dining (right). Generous garlands of fir boughs tangle with climbing vines; small trees in terracotta pots and spruce wreaths on chair backs scent the air with the pungent smell of pine. The intense Prussian blue of the glassware provides the only contrasting shade in this natural bower.

★ The base of the display is a block of florist's oasis trimmed to a conical shape and wrapped in chickenwire for added strength. Attach the oranges (satsumas, clementines or other seasonal fruit) individually with toothpicks, working row by row from the base upwards and fill in the gaps with sprigs of evergreen.

A TOWERING pyramid of oranges in a galvanized metal trough (left) makes a vibrant centrepiece for a Christmas table.

STARK and contemporary, a simple arrangement of protea flowers makes an exotic focal point for an alcove (right). During the winter months, when there are few flowers available for cutting in the garden, such witty displays are a good way of increasing the impact of a few expensive blooms.

★ To achieve the same look, line a clear glass container with bun moss and fill the interior with florists' oasis. Insert the protea stems firmly into the oasis and cover with more moss. The container can be topped up with water from time to time.

A HOSPITABLE array of fruit and nuts in earthenware bowls (above) provides a welcoming sight in a rustic hall. Beneath the polished refectory table large garden tubs are densely packed with dried flowers, including whole roses and gleanings from the hedgerow. Many flowers dry well, particularly those with fine stems. Alchemilla mollis, roses, lavender, hydrangea, heather and cornflowers make a pleasant change from the rather garish everlasting and statice beloved of commercial florists.

★ To air-dry flowers, tie in small bunches and hang upside down in a dark, well-aired room. Roses should be picked just before the flower comes into full bloom.

IN THE Scandinavian Christmas, traces of ancient pagan festivities to celebrate the winter solstice merge with the Christian tradition. Candles, symbolizing the rebirth of the year, are at the centre of many ceremonies. On the Feast of St Lucia, 13 December, which heralds the start of the Christmas season, the daughter of the house is crowned with a lit circle of nine burning candles. For Christmas feasts, specialities of the northern countries include *Julekake*, a honeyed fruit bread, ginger biscuits, salt cod, herring, candied potatoes and ham. With its celebration of light and renewal, and homely fare, the Scandinavian tradition recalls an age-old connection to the land.

STRICTLY for the birds, a nesting box boasts its own festive wreath. Animals are at the heart of the Christmas story. According to legend, at midnight on Christmas Eve, animals gain the power of speech and cattle kneel in honour of Christ's birth. In many countries, it is a tradition to feed farm animals especially well at Christmas to mark their role in the Nativity. Don't forget that midwinter is a lean time for wild visitors to your garden; hang nets of nuts and seeds in tree branches for the birds.

PET OWNERS never fail to indulge their four-legged friends at Christmas, and all children enjoy sharing the spirit of the season with their favourite animals. This miniature fir tree trimmed with dog biscuits is a canine delight; catnip mice would make a good feline alternative. The root ball of the tree is wrapped in moss and damp sacking. Provided the sacking is kept moist, the tree will survive and can be planted and reused the following year.

THE **PERFECT** presentation box for homemade comestibles or a treasure trove of sea shells (left) exploits the textural beauty of natural materials. The woven palm-leaf hamper is gift-wrapped in sage green straw ribbon and trimmed with a raffia bow threaded with a shell.

★ A wide range of humble materials acquire a look of classic elegance when used to decorate Christmas parcels. Cheap upholstery tape, webbing, fine mesh scrim (used by plasterers) and garden twine can be dyed or sprayed, but look equally good in their natural state.

A **SWIRLING** wreath of twigs (right) makes an eye-catching focal point in a Christmas display. The centre of the wreath is decorated with a mound of small cones, walnuts and aromatic cinnamon sticks interspersed with bay leaves and rosemary for pot pourri of seasonal scent.

★ A glue gun (a standard tool in set design, window dressing and styling) is the easiest means of attaching dried ingredients such as nuts and cones to a wreath base. The surface must be relatively flat, clean and dry. A stick of solid glue is fed into the gun, which heats the glue to the right temperature for instant bonding.

CHRISTMAS palates quickly become jaded after days of rich feasting and drinking. To revive flagging appetites, a tempting array of delicacies can be served with coffee at the end of a meal. Dates, dried figs and apricots are standard Christmas accompaniments, as are nuts of every description. For those with a sweet tooth, crystallized fruit is tangy and refreshing.

★ Attach vegetables by wiring in place, or drive thin sharpened garden canes into the bases to hold in position.

THE BASIC form of the wreath invites an imaginative treatment. In winter, colour is in short supply and the rich tints of fresh vegetables supply a useful alternative to flowers. The design of these two wreaths recalls the delightful mélange of the old-fashioned cottage garden, where cabbages compete with roses for growing space. Cream and mauve turnips (above) prove a successful colour match for dried hydrangea heads; while cabbage leaves, radicchio, baby cauliflower, artichokes and lustrous grapes (right) make a cornucopia of delight.

CHESTNUTS to roast on the fire, brazils, walnuts and hazelnuts are neatly segregated in the compartments of an old wooden spice tray (left). As an appetizer with pre-dinner drinks, or to munch while you linger over Stilton and port, nuts are standard Christmas fare.

THE CUP that cheers (right) — everyone has their own favourite recipe for Christmas punch or mulled wine. Serious wine buffs may turn up their noses at spiced wine, but a warming cup of punch is always welcome on a frosty night, a perfect treat for carol-singers or New Year revellers.

★ Traditional spiced wine, popular in Austria and Germany, consists of good red wine warmed with brown sugar and flavoured with whole cinnamon sticks and fruit (oranges, lemons or apples) stuck with cloves. Add a dash of brandy after heating for a stronger drink – and stock up on hangover cures . . .

IF **YOU** invariably return from winter walks with your pockets stuffed with cones, seedpods and other woodland treasures, a wire basket makes an ideal container for displaying your finds. Cinnamon sticks and bay leaves tucked in amongst the cones add the dimension of scent to this simple seasonal arrangement.

FOR **THOSE** who are uncomfortable with the idea of cutting living trees for two weeks' pleasure and who abhor artificial varieties, this twiggy tree (right), crafted in the Far East, provides a natural way of indulging in the Christmas spirit. Decorations echo the mood: simple shapes cut from corrugated card and sprayed gold, clove balls and rustic carved animals and birdhouses complete the look. Strips of toothed corrugated card frame the window, layered at the top to form a pelmet effect.

★ You could create a simpler version of the tree using fewer twigs tacked or glued to a stout central branch. Work from the top downwards, and trim the twigs to shape afterwards – a task for the nimble-fingered.

DECORATE a side table with improvised candle holders. Church candles in pure white come in a wide variety of heights and thicknesses; try beeswax to perfume the air with a sweet scent.

★ Place a pillar candle on your chosen base (the examples shown here use a stack of leaf plates and a cheese box) and anchor with hot wax or a drawing pin pushed through from underneath. Pile up sphagnum moss around each candle to make a soft mound. Decorate with kumquats or bright winter berries.

THE **OVERHANGING** branches of a candlelit chandelier have inspired this festive treatment (above), which brings a touch of the late-season harvests indoors. Russet apples, stored since the autumn, bob overhead, while fir cones dot along the circumference interspersed with twigs. Easy to create and playful, the simplicity of the effect does not overwhelm the plain lines of the chandelier.

A **SMALL BLUE** spruce set in an ornamental terracotta pot (right) is garlanded with swathes of green raffia. An assortment of white candles in clear glass holders makes a magical scene. Blue spruce are among the more costly varieties of Christmas tree, but their dense soft needles (which do not drop) and beautiful colour are well worth the expense. Trees as well-proportioned and lovely as this need little decoration.

S NOWY WHITE linen and sparkling silver set the scene for a
sumptuous Christmas feast. The universal popularity of
turkey as the mainstay of Christmas lunch means that many
people have almost forgotten that there are alternatives. Before
turkey became established, goose was the preferred English
Christmas fare. There are plenty of other rich and robust tastes
to savour at this time of the year. Game is a seasonal choice.
Here roast pheasant is served in the traditional way with
accompanying game chips and a flourish of tail feathers to
decorate the platter.

CANDLES sunk into the top of logs bound with stout twine make a feature of the fireside for a witty rustic look.

★ If you live in an area where wood-burning is permitted, choose logs which give off coloured or scented flames. Applewood, pear and cherry all make sweet-smelling fires, while ash is traditionally the finest fuel of all. Remember that all wood should be dried and seasoned before use; green or wet timber makes poor, smoky and sparky fires.

A BARE HEARTH, especially in winter, is a forlorn sight. If you do not intend to make use of your fireplace, the space can be filled with a festive arrangement which brings cheer and colour to the room (left). Here, the effect of flames is suggested with a variety of bright dried flowers, including roses, supplemented by twigs, moss, and logs, providing a floor-level focal point.

THIS **ELEGANTLY** contrived table decoration (above) assembles a variety of natural materials for a sculptural effect. The candles, in staggered heights, form the focus of the arrangement, while the shallow metal dish is filled with a skilful combination of found ingredients, including driftwood, trails of ivy, poppy seed heads, cones, fir branches and dried lichen, interwoven with a band of muslin. None of these elements is expensive or exotic; many can be found for free.

MASSING is the key to making an impact with simple ingredients. Suggestive of harvest bounty or a generous hospitality, this display on an old stone table (right) uses nothing more unusual than apples and rolled cinnamon sticks bound with raffia to evoke a festive spirit. Flanked by unadorned fir trees in plain terracotta pots and branched ornate candelabra, the effect is reminiscent of feast days in baronial halls.

MAN, **WOMAN** and child in gingerbread summon up the essence of Christmas. Cranberries, bright red checked gingham and Shaker boxes in natural wood add to the homespun appeal.

★ Gingerbread is a perennial Christmas treat everywhere, all the more enjoyable when the family join in the preparations. Spiced biscuits of various descriptions feature in the Christmas customs of many countries, with cinnamon, nutmeg, ginger and cloves being among the favoured flavourings. You can stamp out your gingerbread people with a metal cutter; far more appealing is to cut the dough freehand and add personal touches with icing sugar paste. Children might like to write their names or initials on the biscuits. Make a hole in the top of the cut dough to hang the biscuits on the tree with raffia or ribbon.

S TRUNG over the back of a
rush-bottomed country
chair, an aromatic Shaker
garland made of bay leaves,
dried sliced orange, cinnamon
sticks and ties of blue cotton
threaded on to raffia, looks
good enough to wear. On the
chair seat are arranged the
ingredients for good mulled
wine, including spices wrapped
in little muslin bags, cloves and
cinnamon sticks.

CANDLELIGHT is just as magical outdoors as in – much more evocative than electric light. This church candle (above), spiked on a metal sconce, lights the way to the door, emphasizing the rugged texture of the old stone wall. A fir branch hung over the sconce lends a seasonal touch.

A SIMPLE fir wreath dresses the back of a Shaker chair piled with presents (right). A hydrangea head and balls of lichen bound with forest green satin ribbon add sharp green accents.

★ Bind the branches of fir with twine or wire to achieve a full, rounded shape and wire or tie in the hydrangea heads and lichen balls as contrast. Using the same ribbon on the parcels gives strength to the overall effect.

54

TAMARILLOS in Maryse Boxer plates (left) are set off by a red gingham place mat and crisp white damask napkin. Red is a powerful Christmas colour, bringing vitality and cheerfulness into the home, a reminder of ancient pagan festivities.

LOW centrepieces allow guests to converse freely across the table (right). Sweet chestnuts, green and blue-green fir branches, twigs, apples and a wired red ribbon make a base for a single candle, a long-lasting display to enhance a variety of Christmas festivities from Christmas Eve through to Twelfth Night.

GOLD

GOLD IS LUXURIOUS. Warm and sparkling, it makes the most of dull winter light; in the evening, when the curtains are drawn, the candles lit and fire is burning in the grate, gold adds a glittering dimension of richness and theatricality. Even quite small touches of gold catch the light and multiply its effect.

Ever since the Magi brought their precious gifts, gold has symbolized the generosity of the Christmas season. We continue to give gold in spirit, if not in fact, treating our closest friends and family to special luxuries forsworn the rest of the year. Decorating with gold sets the scene for Christmas splendour and indulgence.

Festive gold baubles, ribbon, trimmings and ornaments fill the shops at Christmas time. With gold paint or spray and a little creativity, it is easy to extend the scope of the theme even further. Dried flowers, leaves, shells, cones and twigs look superb brushed with gold; stencilled stars lift plain tablecloths to heights of Hollywood glamour; sumptuous gold wrapping transforms simple gifts into treasures.

The beauty of decorating with gold lies in its versatility. Rich and splendid on its own, gold is equally effective at enhancing other colours. Elegant and classical with white, warm and enriching paired with red, or in dramatic partnership with black, gold maximizes the impact of Christmas colour schemes. Gold will heighten the refinement of a period room, or lend a graphic edge to a contemporary setting – don't hesitate to go over the top for instant Christmas cheer.

BAROQUE and sumptuous, gold is the richest of all Christmas colours. The glitter of gold provides instant glamour and sophistication in table settings, on the tree or in decorative touches throughout the house. This single gilded pear exemplifies the power of simplicity in Christmas decoration.

I T IS CHRISTMAS EVE and the feast is about to begin. The bare golden tabletop is the perfect base for creating a dazzling and intimate table setting. Each place is lit by a separate candlestick with a starry shade; a heart-shaped tag tied on to the base of the candlestick with picture wire serves as a placement card. Echoing the dramatic black candle shades, each place is set with matte black and gold plates by Maryse Boxer, a black linen napkin bordered in bronze and black twig-handled cutlery. The glasses are intentionally varied; Moroccan style gilded tea glasses partner Murano wine glasses with twisted gold stems. Ridged gold candles in different heights and sizes multiply the light; gold sprayed artichokes in miniature plant pots add an amusing touch. Gold-wrapped chocolate at each plate inaugurates the start of the gift-giving season.

★ The warm glow of candlelight enhances the richness of the gold theme. Shade each candle individually to emphasize the sense of intimacy.

GOLD lends impact to the simplest ingredients. This elegant black and gold place setting (left) comprises a black linen napkin bordered with metallic bronze and silver edging, bound up with a twist of gilt mesh, and a placement card made from a large leaf sprayed gold.

★ Gold trimmings are not difficult to find, particularly at Christmas time. Ribbon, braid, scraps of brocade, gimp and fringing make impromptu napkin ties or borders. For added interest, play up the textural contrast of shiny metallic and dulled antiqued finishes.

DIVINELY decadent, exotic wrapping in black and gold makes a present fit for a diva (right). The box is covered in gold tissue paper, enveloped in a frothy cloud of black tulle and tied up with gold and black ribbon.

★ Tulle, widely available in a vast range of colours, adds a touch of theatricality to any special gift. It is inexpensive, so you can afford to be generous with the amount. Gather the tulle together at the top of the parcel and tie so that the material stands up in stiff folds.

★ Gold leaves for trimming parcels and gifts can be constructed out of metal foil available from craft shops. Trace around a real leaf to make a paper pattern of the shape to use as a guide. Place the pattern on the foil, score around the outside with a sharp point and cut out the shape. Use the sharp point (a compass end, nail, or the points of scissors) to mark the surface of the foil with a pattern of veining.

HOMEMADE presents are always appreciated. Glazed grapes, pears and plums (above), packed with golden baubles in a cellophane wrapper, make a perfect hostess gift.

A **MIRROR** reflects the sheen of gilded decoration and multiplies the flickering points of candlelight, in a dramatic display for an entrance hall. A wreath of golden laurel leaves (right) hangs over a gilt-framed mirror, lit by an ornate candelabra. Presents wrapped in shiny gold paper tied up with cord, tangerines, gold baubles and pine cones pursue the theme.

★ A wreath of laurel leaves was the ancient Greek token of victory and remains a symbol of honour and nobility. Laurel wreaths are particularly effective in a period setting, where they complement the classical elegance of architectural detail. The sturdy laurel leaf is ideal for spraying; gold spray is widely available from craft shops and easy to use. To recreate the same effect, wire the stems of sprayed leaves on to a moss-covered wreath base. Overlap each cluster for even coverage and arrange the leaves so that they all point in the same direction. As an alternative, you could also make the wreath using preserved magnolia leaves, which range in colour from dull red to near black.

★ To make a pear shape in papier mâché, use a balloon partly blown up or a real pear (unripe) as a base for modelling. After the papier mâché has dried, make a small hole in the top, burst the balloon and remove; or cut the shape in half to remove the pear and glue back together again. Decorate with acrylic paint or 'Dutch' gold leaf, a cheaper version of the traditional variety.

PLAYFULLY transformed, garden pots and spirals of wire make original Christmas centrepieces (above). The tree-shape of the wire plant supports suggest the theme; cut-out metal birds and leaves are suspended from the skeletal forms. The bases of the terracotta pots are filled with mounds of spongy reindeer moss, a type of dried lichen. Candleholders are improvised from smaller pots painted gold and similarly filled with reindeer moss. The effect is of stark simplicity, made festive by the judicious use of gold and candlelight.

ON THE FIRST DAY of Christmas, my true love gave to me . . . a partridge in a pear tree. This witty interpretation of the traditional Christmas song (right) makes a delightful alternative to an evergreen tree. The tree trunk is a fallen T-shaped branch, with a forest of bare twigs pushed into a series of holes drilled along the upper edge forming the 'branches'. The partridge, nestling in the centre of the tree, and the gilt pears which hang from the branches are made of papier mâché. Dried lotus heads and star anise are flecked with gold paint.

GIFTS with an imaginative twist – original ideas for wrapping up presents add to the excitement and anticipation (above). Only those with extraordinary powers of self control can refrain from trying to guess the contents of all those intriguing packages under the tree. It is sometimes wise to wait and put parcels of giveaway shapes and sizes on display only as Christmas Eve draws near, or to disguise the gift with its packaging. A brown paper parcel tied up with lashings of string is plainly mysterious, while the mock-crocodile shoebox with shoe horn tied on top gives the game away. Sober and elegant, a present handsomely wrapped in forest green leaf paper delicately overprinted in gold is trimmed with a trail of ivy. Glass paper, gold gauze ribbon and ropes of pearls advertise what must certainly be a luxurious gift.

SO **MANY** of the celebrations at Christmas time centre around food that it is worth making a special effort to transform the table into a focus of attention. A table beautifully set and decorated whets the appetite just as effectively as tempting aromas from the kitchen. This table setting (right) marries inherited glass and china with modern decorations; touches of gold add a note of elegance and festivity. The table is covered with a starched damask cloth, the epitome of simple luxury. Gilded shells and starfish serve as napkin rings, while simple terracotta pots painted gold make containers for flowers and food. The base of each setting is a plain white china plate with a gilded edge;' antique china and glass add interest and individuality. This serendipitous approach gives a charming but informal feeling to the table and helps to put guests at their ease.

★ Before electric light, burning candles flickered on the branches of Christmas trees. According to legend, it was Martin Luther who began the practice, the candles supposedly a reminder of the starry night sky. Candlelit trees obviously pose a considerable risk of fire and most people today are content with electrical substitutes. Nevertheless, the magical beauty of candlelight can still be enjoyed provided care is taken to ensure that the candles are firmly supported and set away from any material which could easily be set alight. Common sense dictates that any display which includes burning candles should never be left unattended.

A DRAMATIC tree of candles (above) makes a golden focal point for a Christmas Eve party. The plain white candles are spiked on to a tiered shaped stand; dripping wax cascades down the side. Groups of three roses cut low are placed around the base of the display, encircled by a wreath of evergreen.

THE EXTRAVAGANCE of Baroque interiors, enriched with carved and gilded ornamentation and echoing to the strains of chamber music, is evoked in the golden decoration of this Christmas tree (left). Here, scrolls of sheet music bound with ribbon festoon the branches of the tree, accompanied by gold-wrapped miniature violins, bead chains, gilt urns and clove-studded oranges. Dull gold brocade spills in generous folds on the floor to complete the lustrous, antique look.

★ Adopting a theme, which can be emphasized by the choice of colours, lends impact to decoration, as well as wit and charm. Try gold cherubs, stars and trumpets for a celestial theme, shells sprayed gold and fish shapes cut from metal foil for a nautical flavour.

COMBINE gold with ruby red for a look of mellow richness (above). Gold string balls act as a foil for the warm tones of claret-filled glasses and etched antique decanter.

★ Gold catches the eye and reflects the light. Twists of wired gold ribbon or mesh can be tied around the stems of glasses, on banisters, on the branches of the tree, on wreaths or even on chair backs to make a simple festive gesture.

WATER and candlelight make an irresistible combination. Small golden flower candles floating in a heavy round Steuben dish (left) provide a strikingly simple decoration with an Eastern flavour for the dining table or entrance hall.

A **FROSTED** glass bowl decorated with stars and filled with gold sugared almonds is newly unveiled from its wrapping of gold tissue and gilt mesh ribbon (left). Gold spray, crystals and tiny bunches of glass fruit transform a wrought iron candlestick. Miniature gold paper crackers enclose sweets and favours.

★ Gild baskets, dried hydrangea heads, seed pods and cones with spray; apply paint to cover pots, wooden trays and boxes. Metallic pens can be used to provide a flourish of gold on plain brown wrapping paper, or to decorate a length of lining paper for an instant table cover.

A **DELECTABLE** tea-time table setting for Christmas Day (right) combines a gold-printed cloth and napkin with a gold heart-shaped plate. Delicious German stollen cake, rich with fruit and almonds, is a traditional treat.

Gold can suggest many moods, from the height of Hollywood glamour to the refinement of grand period rooms. Here, a block of wood sprayed gold serves as a coffee tray for a Harlequin cup and saucer (above). The bold flat planes of colour have a graphic, contemporary feel.

An eighteenth-century gilded fireplace inspires an eccentric flight of Christmas fancy (left). Grisaille cherubs cavorting on a frescoed wall burnished with gold, and bronze cherubs on the cast-iron fireback suggest an angelic theme. Gilt cherubs and loops of gold beads are suspended over the fireplace from picture hooks; the mantelshelf arrangement mixes plaster casts of angel heads, gold and glass Christmas tree balls and candles in staggered heights set in antiqued candlesticks. An idiosyncratic collection of enchanting painted paper figures invite closer scrutiny on the bookshelves.

W H I T E

I N MY MEMORY, Christmas was always white. After the drab months of November and December, we are ready for a shimmering, sparkling Christmas to lift our spirits. When nature plays her part, when the ground lies covered with a deep mantle of snow and frost brings a cruel glamour to the garden, the world is magically transformed.

If the snowflakes stubbornly refuse to fall and a white Christmas remains a dream, we can still recapture the brilliance and glitter of the winter landscape indoors. In this section I have combined the light, bright colours of silver, white and frost that work so well together. Opalescent and crystalline, they recreate the dazzling effect of light reflected from snow and ice.

Most of us already have a lot of white in our homes – table linen and china, glass and silverware. To these basic elements can be added gauze ribbon, crystal drops, glass ornaments, pearly balls and beads to create beautiful table settings or to dress a tree.

The Christmas rose and the snowdrop, two of the few flowers properly in season at this time of year, contribute a delicate purity in winter arrangements; while the silvery foliage of spruce and eucalyptus are naturally complementary. Twigs, leaves and cones can be lightly sprayed or painted for a seasonal frosted look.

Silver is a very cold colour and certainly reflects the temperature outside, but it is also sophisticated and ethereal. White is stylish, modern and romantic. Together they bring elegance and eye-catching distinction to a room, as well as adding sparkle and flair to the party season, whatever the weather is like.

S ILVER glitters like the icy winter landscape. Eye-catching and amusing, chocolate sardines wrapped in silver paper make a shimmering wreath to hang on the door. The wreath base is covered with bunched up green tissue paper, glued in place; the sardines are secured on top, with their heads all pointing in the same direction. An iridescent bow adds a final flourish. Experimenting with unusual and unexpected ingredients brings a playful approach to Christmas decoration.

★ Ivy is an indispensable winter foliage, associated with Christmas and winter festivals since the earliest times. There are many different varieties of leaf shape and size, and colours range from golden to deep glossy green. Ivy is cheap to buy, but most gardens generally have some ivy growing in a corner, trailing over a wall or clambering up a tree trunk which can be cut for free and brought indoors to form the basis for garlands and wreaths. Ivy trails are long-lasting even out of water.

THE TRANQUILLITY and refinement of an all-white room is echoed in the elegant restraint of these Christmas decorations (above). Over a painted white fireplace, a simple garland of ivy is festooned with large crystal drops. Presents are wrapped in different types of silver paper and trimmed with twists of silver foil.

A SUPERB winter garland brings a look of abundance to a contemporary fireside (right). White roses, green apples, holly, spruce and cinnamon sticks bound with twists of white muslin complement the carefully judged neutral tones of the decorative scheme.

★ To make a garland which includes fresh flowers, you must provide a supply of water. Here, the central arrangement of white roses is constructed using a large block of florist's oasis set in a tray or shallow dish. Oasis is available in different sizes and shapes and must be thoroughly soaked in water before use. The stems of the fresh flowers can be inserted into the porous material and will take up the water they need provided the dish is regularly topped up.

F ROSTED glass balls, Mexican tin ornaments and a Murano glass sun are suspended from a rope of white pearls to make a glittering garland to hang on the tree or against the frosted window pane.

★ Silver paste trimmings, pearlized baubles, glass beads, fake pearls and crystal drops can all be found in antique markets or junk shops to supply the ingredients for a white theme. Tin ornaments are widely available in shops selling ethnic crafts, or you can make your own by cutting simple shapes out of sheets of tin. Use a small hammer or nailhead to dent the surface with a pattern of dots or score lines with the end of a knitting needle or similar spiked tool.

FEW FLOWERS, apart from the snowdrop, appear in the garden during the depths of winter. For those who simply can't wait for spring, potted bulbs, brought on early in the greenhouse, speak of warmer days to come (above). Generous cotton handkerchiefs wrap the pots of these spring bulbs; moss packed around the base of the stems suggest the effect of natural growth.

WHITE FLOWERS, grouped on a window sill, are bathed in pale wintry sunshine (left). The large display, arranged in a frosted vase, consists of a generous bunch of Christmas roses (*Helleborus niger*), interspersed with fruited ivy; to the left is a small posy of delicate snowdrops. A beaten pewter candlestick and a selection of silver, glass and iridescent balls complete the picture.

★ Christmas roses, traditional in seasonal arrangements, have beautiful waxy petals and prominent golden stamens. Although they are expensive to buy, the flowers last a long time. The fragility of snowdrops, another popular winter flower, calls for simplicity in display. Stems are too short and frail to be inserted in oasis; display in low vases or bowls.

HOMEMADE petits fours nestling in paper baking cases (left) round off a meal with a light touch. An old wooden seed box lined with hand trimmed paper makes an innovative and charming serving tray.

★ Ordinary waxed or parchment baking paper can be given the look of the finest broderie anglaise by scalloping the edges of the sheets and making a series of holes with a punch. Fold each sheet of paper in half first for symmetrical edges.

FROSTED plums, apricots and grapes in a Victorian glass dish (right) make a centrepiece for the table which is delicious to eat. The Venetian mirror in the background could be laid flat under the bowl to add sparkle to the table and reflect light upwards.

★ Frosted fruit is easy to do and can be made well in advance of the Christmas rush. Choose fruit which is quite firm, not at the peak of ripeness. Brush each piece with the white of an egg and sprinkle with caster sugar. Any bare patches can be touched up individually using a fine sable brush. Leave in the refrigerator overnight to harden.
The petals of edible flowers, such as roses, can also be frosted. Use a fine brush to paint both sides of each petal with egg white and coat with sugar. Dry in an airing cupboard for a day and store in a cool place between layers of waxed paper.

STARK and contemporary, a wire cage encloses a single white church candle set in a simple metal holder. With the lights turned low, the gridded shadows cast by the metal mesh add pattern to plain walls.

★ Chickenwire, the stock in trade of professional florists, is light and malleable and can be manipulated into a variety of shapes to make improvised bases for candles. Galvanized watering cans and small shiny tin pails make original containers for winter flower arrangements; use a large metal pail as a cachepot for a Christmas tree.

A **LIBRARY** lamp, with a base shaped like a piece of driftwood, is trimmed with a single Christmas ball hung on a silvery ribbon. Christmas balls in clear, frosted or opalescent glass, silver glitter, faceted mirror, or smooth pale silk ring the changes on the elegant white theme.

★ For electrical safety out of doors, ensure that the lights, cable and power sockets you use are designed to be weather-proof.

★ Winter is not a time to linger outside, but if your dining room overlooks the garden, outdoor lighting will transform the view from the table.

FIREWORKS make a fountain of light on New Year's Eve (above). Candles in glass lantern jars pick out a flight of stone steps with light, leading the way to the festivities.

TWINKLING fairy lights strung over the arches of a rose arbour (right) extend seasonal good wishes to guests and neighbours. Lights to decorate a fir tree, to frame a doorway or trail along the edge of a balcony express the Christmas spirit. Strings of a single-coloured lights are elegant and stylish; focus on a single point of interest for maximum impact.

★ White tissue must rank among the most economical of wrapping papers. Use in generous layers to conceal the present effectively. For extra sparkle, glue on individual sequins or foil rosettes. You can also brush the paper lightly with glue and scatter glitter over the top or decorate with silver felt pens.

ETHEREAL and romantic, white-on-white is the summit of style. A present wrapped in layers of white tissue paper covered in a cloud of tulle (above) is tied up with silver ribbon and finished with an old sequined bow.

ALL-WHITE Christmas trees have a fairytale magic that recalls a snowy woodland scene. Opalescent glass balls (left), like soap bubbles, are combined with bows of silver ribbon, frothy white tulle, silvered eucalyptus and pine cones and white rose beads. Tiny white Christmas candles are secured in metal clips.

★ Seedpods, cones and leaves can be frosted with silver spray paint available from art shops. Alternatively, you can tip cones with ordinary white paint. Eucalyptus, lichen, and blue spruce are naturally silvery grey and complement a white theme. Insert rose stems in florist's vials to prolong their life and keep topped up daily with water.

TURKISH DELIGHT (above), powdered with sugar, is served on a mother-of-pearl shell-shaped dish – an exotic sweetmeat that was nearly the undoing of Edmund, as lovers of the magical Narnia stories will recall. Marrons glacés and crystallized ginger are equally tempting to nibble with after-dinner coffee.

CUT GLASS and polished silver multiply the reflections for a sparkling Christmas table setting (left). White roses and lilies make an elegant centrepiece, the sides of the flower container swathed in dotted voile. Strings of tiny silver stars loop over crystal candlesticks; an etched glass bowl is piled with glittering ornaments. Silver stars and twig-handled cutlery are arranged on a snowy cloth faintly patterned with stars.

★ If you do not number a damask cloth among your treasured possessions, improvise white table covers from lengths of crisp white sheeting or billows of muslin over a plain undercloth, draped or swagged generously at the corners. For a hint of decoration, cut out a stencil from a piece of stiff card and spray silver stars in a sparse pattern over the cloth, or dot with tiny star stickers.

COLOUR

DECORATING A ROOM in vivid colours is the most immediate way of saying that Christmas has come. Bright colour instantly puts me in a holiday mood and brings out my *joie de vivre*. Each year I choose a different colour theme for all my decorations – for the tree, wrapping paper, tags, ribbon, flowers and candles. Strict coordination can look lifeless and contrived, but working with a limited palette of vibrant clashing colours is brilliant and fun.

Colour is uplifting and festive at any time of the year. In midwinter, when skies are often grey and overcast and evenings are long, it is twice as powerful and enriching. Many of us fight shy of choosing strong colours when it comes to painting the walls and furnishing our homes, for fear we will grow tired of them.

Christmas is the one time of the year when we can indulge in a little fantasy and let our imaginations run wild. In the season of pantomime and gala occasions, when costumes and stage scenery glow with luminous hues, bright colour brings a touch of theatricality into the home.

Red is the quintessential Christmas colour, and red and green are the traditional pairing. As children we made thick paperchains in paintbox colours which were looped up over our heads from the picture rails. Today, there is no need to restrict our choice to red and green or to primaries. Intense shades such as cerise pink, ultramarine, saffron yellow and lime green are fresh and exciting and bring new life to Christmas traditions. No holding back!

MOUTHWATERING crystallized fruits in a cut glass bowl make a colourful focal point for a sideboard or buffet table. The practice of candying or crystallizing fruit originated in Italy and first became popular in Britain in Tudor and Stuart times. Centuries before refrigeration or canning, crystallizing was a means of preserving the bounty of the summer months to provide delicacies for winter feasts. The petals of edible flowers, as well as herbs, vegetables and many kinds of fruit were treated in this way.

THE **VIBRANT** clashing shades of these pencil-thin tapers (above) are shown to advantage in a galvanized jug. Colour is revitalizing, instantly festive. Instead of the safe Christmas combination of red and green, ring the changes with accessories and details in hot, bright shades – acid yellow, pink, magenta and lime green – for the shock of the new.

A **CHRISTMAS** tree, decorated especially for the children, provides a magical sight in the nursery (right). Children are great traditionalists when it comes to Christmas decorations and love to see their old favourites on the tree year after year; providing them with their own tree to trim leaves you free to adopt a more original approach elsewhere in the house. A toyshop theme has perennial appeal; here, teddies and a selection of bright paper stars, hearts and chains looks cheerful and busy.

★ Children like to display their handiwork and participate in all the preparations. Paper decorations are cheap and easy for young fingers to fashion. To make concertina paper chains, take two long strips of paper in contrasting colours and glue at one end so the strips form a right-angle. Then fold each strip over the other in turn. For a garland of paper bows, fan pleat small pieces of crêpe paper and tie on to coloured string.

PRESENTS are especially delightful when they have been wrapped to reflect the personality of their recipient. Pale pink tulle over contrasting tissue paper, tied with a vivid grosgrain ribbon, adds a touch of romance to a gift for a young girl. The delicate pink and gold tablecloth by Carolyn Quatermaine was inspired by an eighteenth century book of calligraphy and printed with hearts and French sayings.

★ Lengths of tartan, brocade or sumptuous silk all make good festive table covers and may be swagged and tasselled at the corners or hung simply over a contrasting underskirt. Search out upholstery shops or fabric stalls for interesting remnants. Saris, brilliantly patterned or shot with glittering gold or silver thread, provide instant glamour draped over a table.

ACID **DROPS** in a Victorian glass bowl and striped sugar cane (left) make a tempting display for those with a sweet tooth. Homemade sweets in crinkly cellophane bags tied up with ribbon are delightful party favours to have on hand for Christmas guests. Fudge, nougat, peppermint creams and marzipan are all simple edible gifts to make in your own kitchen.

AN **ARRAY** of crystallized and frosted fruits (right) a provides visual feast. Chocolate-covered fruit is a simple and luxurious alternative. Use a toothpick to dip tangerine segments or black grapes into melted chocolate and allow to cool and harden.

★ Sweetmeats of various descriptions make a colourful theme for decorating a tree. Bags of gold chocolate money, gaudy foil-wrapped sweets, marzipan shapes threaded on a loop of braid, iced ginger biscuits and dried fruit are irresistible and indulgent.

THESE CHEERFUL spotty
Christmas balls and papier
mâché animals are bright
with paintbox colour.

★ Papier mâché ornaments are
quick and easy to do, and small
children will have fun with this
messy activity. You need a supply
of newspaper, torn into strips,
and either wallpaper or
flour-and-water paste. Make the
balls by covering small balloons
with strips of paper soaked in
paste. After these have dried,
burst the balloons and decorate
with bright acrylic paint – acrylic
is fast-drying to a bright finish
and water-soluble, which makes
clearing up easier. Trim with
polka dot ribbon.

THE RICH and sophisticated shades of russet, dull gold and antique red emphasize the cosiness of this Christmas fireside. The strength of the effect relies on a limited palette of colours, repeated in the gift wrapping, trimming and mantelpiece garland. Contorted willow branches are sparsely decorated with small bunches of dried rosebuds, pomegranates and glossy black berries. Presents, simply wrapped in plain paper and bound with raffia, or hidden from inquisitive eyes in sumptuous velvet sacks tied up with satin ribbon, are ready for Christmas morning.

CHRISTMAS begins at daybreak with the thrilling discovery of treats and presents spilling out of stockings and pillowcases. North American children hang their stockings by the fireside, Dutch children leave out their shoes on St Nicholas Eve, but in Britain stockings or (more hopefully) pillowcases are usually hung at the end of the bed on Christmas Eve. This brass bedstead (above) sports two hessian sacks, decorated with tiny colourful bows, tied on with contrasting ribbons. The bedhead, trimmed with evergreen boughs and brightly-coloured silk flowers and berries, completes the festive bedroom.

THE **SHEER** exuberance of colour is instantly appealing. A child's place setting (left) combines a brilliant blue heart plate with a Mexican tin reindeer, chocolate crocodile, vivid Christmas tree ball and Smarties mischievously scattered over the table.

★ To transform a basic kitchen table for a Christmas or New Year's party, you can wrap the top in thick, bright paper, taping the edges underneath. Alternatively, buy a roll of cheap white lining paper and decorate with stencilled stars, leaves, hearts or spots.

THE **STRIKING** contrast of yellow and blue Maryse Boxer plates, shocking pink bauble and placement card (right) exploits the intensity of complementary colours. The pairing of blue and yellow, red and green, yellow and pink are naturally vibrant and exciting — too intense, perhaps, for most people to live with every day; but superb for lifting the spirits and creating an atmosphere of celebration.

FABBRICA DI CIOCCOLATA

Rivoire

VIA VACCHERECCIA, 4 r.

FIRENZE

GROOVY patterns (above) transform a simple display of citrus fruit on a curly wire stand into an unusual Christmas centrepiece.

★ Choose any citrus fruit – oranges, lemons, limes, green grapefruit and tangerines – and score lines into the peel using a sharp canelle knife. The display will last for a good week. A special bonus is the sharp refreshing citrus scent.

BLOCKS of chocolate wrapped in primary shades (left) make good stocking fillers and provide a simple means of adding a splash of colour around the house – in a guest room, on a hall table or piled on a desk in a study. Small bowls of Amaretti biscuits, with their gaily coloured paper wrappers, are another personal favourite. Christmas is traditionally a time to indulge in life's luxuries.

EXPERIMENTING with colour allows you to break free from tradition. Don't be afraid to mix shapes and textures or objects from different periods and cultures. This table setting combines antique crystal, modern Murano glass, bright ceramics, harlequin Staffordshire cups, Mexican tin decorations, Indian napkins and tassels to striking effect. Christmas tree ornaments look just as decorative piled in a bowl or square glass vase as they do on the tree. The exotic trumpet flowers of amaryllis provide a dash of colour.

★ Amaryllis, available throughout the winter months, either as cut flowers or potted plants, have long fleshy stems and dramatic white, red or pink flowers. Although expensive, they are very long-lasting, and once the stems have begun to soften, you can cut the flowers low and display in a shallow bowl to prolong the enjoyment.

FROM AN EARLY age, children can participate in a wide range of Christmas preparations; making cards, decorations and homemade presents is a constructive way of looking forward to the festivities. This miniature carrier bag was designed and made by my daughter, Charlotte Rose, who was especially pleased with the plaited handles.

★ A handmade Christmas card has much more meaning than its commercial counterpart and children rarely need much encouragement to come up with their own designs. Images from last year's cards can be saved to cut up for collages; shells, glitter, sequins, tin ornaments and pressed flowers used for decoration. For making cards in greater numbers, stencilled designs or potato prints are easy and cheap, or you can photocopy a line drawing for individual handcolouring later.

BEAUTIFULLY wrapped presents are a pleasure to receive and contribute their own decorative interest piled under the tree. An imaginative and original effect does not depend on expensive wrapping paper and trimmings – with cheaper ingredients, you can afford to be more lavish. These parcels are wrapped in layers of inexpensive bright tissue paper, banded with contrasting colours and trimmed with Christmas decorations. Ribbon with wired edges can be crinkled and tweaked into shape for a lively look. The overall efffect is of fun, frivolity and seasonal good cheer.

117

★ Antique markets, junk shops and old-fashioned haberdashers are good hunting grounds for all kinds of inexpensive trimmings, including tassels, paste bows, antique glass beads, snippets of ribbon and brocade, all of which can provide a starting point for your decorative ideas.

BRIGHTLY coloured tassels and Christmas tree ornaments strung together (above) make an eye-catching garland to hang against the light over a window pane or dangle on the tree.

COLOURED fairy lights (left) make illuminating the tree a safe prospect, generating negligible amounts of heat. There's something innately cheering about these twinkling points of colour. Indispensable on the tree, fairy lights work equally well twined through garlands or wreaths. Multicoloured lights have a childlike appeal; single coloured strands are stylish.

PICTURE CREDITS

Special Photography: Tony Amos
14, 18-19, 22, 23, 31, 32, 33, 34-35, 40, 42-43, 52, 53, 56, 57, 58, 60-61, 62, 63, 72, 74, 75, 77, 82-83, 87, 88, 89, 93, 95, 100-101, 104-105, 106, 110, 111, 112, 113, 114-115, 116, 117, 119;

The Publisher would like to thank the following for their kind permission to reproduce photographs in this book:

Anthony Blake Photo Library 39, 46-47, /Kieran Scott 102

David Burch 38;

Camera Press 20-21, 99;

IPC Magazines/Robert Harding Syndication 16, 44, 66, /Jan Baldwin 55, /Henry Bourne 24, 25, 45, /Simon Brown 94-95, /Christopher Drake 67, 107, /Robin Matthews 70, /Les Meehan 41, 49, /James Merrell 6 top left and bottom left, 13, 36, 37, 78, 84, 109, /George Ong 85, /Simon Page-Ritchie 98, /Debbie Patterson 26, /Jonathon Pilkington 48, /Peter Rauter 68, 76, /Trevor Richards 6 top right, 92, /Paul Ryan 28-29, /Debi Treloar 80, 81, 108, /Pia Tryde 64, 86, 103, /Simon Wheeler 69;

Jerry Harpur 91;

Marianne Majerus 30, 90 (designer: George Carter), /Good Housekeeping/The National Magazine Company 71

S & O Mathews 96;

Alan Newnham 73;

Gill Orsman 1, 118

Elizabeth Whiting & Associates /Tim Beddow 9, /Tommy Candler 17, /Di Lewis 2, 6 bottom right, 27 (designer: Jane Parker), 50, 65, /Tim Street-Porter 29 right (designer: Eve Steele), /Simon Upton 54 (Faulkner and McGregor), Victor Watts 51.

Pavilion Books would like to thank the following London stores for their assistance in providing props for this book:

Liberty, Regent Street, London W1 (tel: 071 734 1234)
Props used on pages 40, 74, 60-1, 84

Thomas Goode, 19 South Audley Street, London W1 (tel: 071 499 2823)
Props used on pages 60-1, 62, 74, 75, 77

Maryse Boxer and Carolyn Quatermaine, Chez Joseph, 26 Sloane Street, London SW1 (tel: 071 245 9493)
Props used on pages 23, 18-19, 56, 60-1, 74, 75, 100-1, 104-5, 110, 111

The Shaker Shop, 322 Kings Road, London SW3 (tel: 071 352 3918)
Props used on pages 14, 18-19, 52-3

Designers Guild, 271 Kings Road, London SW3 (tel: 071 351 5775)
Props used on pages 18-19, 42-3, 112-3